History of the Church of
The Most Holy Redeemer

Eagle Harbor, Michigan

SESQUI-CENTENNIAL
1854-2004

By

Robert F. Carlton

Robert F. Carlton (author) and Bishop James H. Garland
150th Anniversary of The Most Holy Redeemer Church
Eagle Harbor, MI   25 July 2004
PHOTO CREDIT: Kathleen Carlton Johnson

The Most Holy Redeemer Church
Photograph by Forster

The Most Holy Redeemer Church
Wood Carving by Elmer L Johnson

The Most Holy Redeemer Church
Sketch by Alice Reynolds

The Most Holy Redeemer Church
Painting by Alice Reynolds

Dedicated to all the Priests
that have served at
The Most Holy Redeemer Church
Eagle Harbor, Michigan
and nourished the faithful with the
Most Holy Eucharist
1854 - 2023

Table of Contents

Illustrations and Photos

Acknowledgments

Data compilation

This bit of history of Holy Redeemer is compiled from many sources, much of the 19th century data was extracted from "History of the Diocese of Sault Ste. Marie and Marquette" by Rt. Rev. Msgr. Antoine Ivan Rezek, LLD, a two volume works that was published in 1906.

1 Rt. Rev. Msgr. Antoine Ivan Rezek, LLD
PHOTO CREDIT
Msgr. Rezek's "History of the Diocese of Sault Ste. Marie and Marquette - 1906"

Additional data was compiled from the following:

1. "Preaching the Gospel Anew, Saint Clement Maria Hofbauer"
    by Josef Heinzmann, C.Ss.R.

2. "Shepherd of the Wilderness" by Bernard J. Lambert.

3. "The Apostle of the Chippewa's" by Joseph Gregorich.

4. "Cross and Anchor" by Jamison.

5. "P'ere Marquette" by Agnes Repplier.

6. "Missionary Labors of Fathers Marquette, Menard and Allouez in the Lake Superior Region" by Rev. Chrysostom Verwyst, O.S.F.

7. "Early History of Gollschee-Kocevje-Carniola" by Edward Skender.

8.   "Lake Superior" by Grace Lee Nute.

9.   Catholic Encyclopedia.

10. Bishop Baraga Association and Archives, Elizabeth Delene, Archivist.

11. Franciscan Archives, Cincinnati, Fr. Dan Anderson O.F.M.

12. Archives of University of Notre Dame.

13. Archives of Marquette University.

14. Michigan Tech Archives and Copper Country Historical Collection, Erik Nordberg, Archivist.

15. Mrs. Frances (Schuler) Rozich, Keweenaw County Historian.

16. "Delaware, Michigan its History," Clarence J. Monette, Historian and Publisher.

17. National Park Service, National Register of Historic Places, Listing on the National Record.

18. 1934 Souvenir of Holy Redeemer Church by Fr. Bonaventure Kilfoyle, O.F.M., Pastor.

19. Bishop Baraga Mission Souvenir Holy Redeemer Church by Fr. Juniper Hukenbeck, O.F.M., Pastor 1934 - 1944.

20. "Franciscan Missionaries Now Labor in Mission Founded by Fr. Baraga" by Frs. Jordon Telles, O.F.M. and Clarence Tittel, O.F.M., as published in the Northern Michigan Edition of Our Sunday Visitor, 30 June 1953.

21. Correspondence with Fr. John McArdle of Menominee, MI

22. Correspondence with Fr. Miles Pfalzer, O.F.M. of Easton, PA.

23. Correspondence with Fr. Ed Lammert, O.F.M. of Cumberland, KY.

24. E-mail from Fr. Matthew Krempel, O.F.M., Calexico, CA.

25. Letter from Mary Claire Smith to Joseph Gregorich dated 27 September 1955.

26. Oral history, interview with the following:
    Mrs. Frances Schuler Rozich|
    Mr. Paul Foley
    Fr. Ed Lammert, O.F.M.
    Fr. Tom Schmied, O.F.M., Cap.
    Fr. Sebastion Ettolil, M.C.B.S.
    Mr. John Landreville

27. Fr. Wayne Marcotte, Pastor, Church of the Resurrection, Hancock.

28. Marilyn Winquist, Clerk, Keweenaw County.

29. John Kezel, Keweenaw Catholic Missions, Secretary.

30. Calumet Public Library, Librarian Debra Oyler, and staff.

31. Theresa C. Clevenstine, Chisholm, MN, Western Lake Superior and Iron Range Research.

32. Kathleen C. Johnson, Librarian, General Research.

33. Elmo J. Negro, Keweenaw County Mine Locations.

34. Sharon Rozich, Copying.

Technical assistance and logistics:

35. Bob and Mary Kay Masnado, Sexton, and assistant.

36. Robbie Johnson Computer Techniques.

37. Regina Johnson Computer Techniques.

38. Peggy Carlton, my right hand, and helper during the eight months required to research and write this bit of history.

Updated and reprinted in 2023.

39. Keweenaw Catholic Community.

40. Bishop Baraga Association, Marquette MI.

Introduction

by Fr. Sebastian Ettolil MCBS, Pastor

We are preparing to celebrate the 150th anniversary of the Most Holy Redeemer Church in Eagle Harbor, Michigan. At this historic moment I am happy to introduce this interesting and detailed history of the Most Holy Redeemer Church to the public in commemoration of the anniversary. I appreciate Mr. Robert Carlton's arduous work of research to compile this valuable book in gratitude to all the priests who served this church. The anniversary celebration is set for July 25th, 2004, presided by Most Rev. James Garland, Bishop of Marquette.

The Holy Redeemer Church, Eagle Harbor had the great beginning with Bishop Frederic Baraga. Father Baraga began visiting Eagle Harbor in 1846 to preach to settlers and Indians. After his appointment as the first Bishop of Upper Michigan in 1853 he sent Fr. Henry L. Thiele to Eagle Harbor to serve the parish. The church was built in 1854 under the new priest's direction. The list of priests assigned to this parish is found in this book. From 1905 the Franciscan Fathers began to serve and recently from 2001 the Fathers of the Missionary Congregation of the Blessed Sacrament from India are serving here.

The church is a fine example of braced frame construction built of white pine. It features a tower with louvered belfry and octagonal spire. Bishop Baraga's original pulpit and altar are preserved here. The interior features include the altar with antique chandelier. Bishop Baraga's vestments, chalice and missal are on display at the rear. Bishop died on January 19, 1868. The remains are interred in the crypt of St. Peter Cathedral Marquette, Michigan. In 1930 a group of Slovenian Catholics in the Chicago area began the Bishop Baraga Association to promote the knowledge and life of Bishop Baraga and to promote his canonization. The official cause for canonization opened in 1952 and has made steady progress.

In 1986 and 2003 much needed repairs and renovation were done to the church. We acknowledge gratefully all who contribute generously with this project. Every year the church is visited by many tourists from here and abroad. The visitors' book is a good record of appreciation of visitors. During the 2000 Jubilee Year this church was designated by the diocese as a place of pilgrimage for the Holy Year. Now this church is used for summer service with Mass on Sundays at 9:00 A.M.

Those that have gone before us have done a great job and they have left us a rich heritage. It is our privilege and duty to continue that heritage. We are grateful to the dedicated priest and faithful. May this anniversary fill us with God's Blessings and continued growth of the church.

Foreword

This brief history of Holy Redeemer Church, Eagle Harbor has been compiled from many documented sources and from the personal memories of this writer. Several historical facts related to Holy Redeemer are also captured here as:

1. The story of Father Jacker who served at Eagle Harbor on several occasions, takes some twist through the local area as well as in the realm of Father Jacques Marquette.

2. The reason Father A. Molinari was assigned to Holy Redeemer and its ties to local history.

3. Buckeye Barracks, the old Delaware boarding house as it relates to a visiting priest that has celebrated Mass here each summer for past forty years.

In spite of the hardships our predecessors went through in the era prior to modern utilities, transportation and communication, they managed to attend to the Sacraments by any means at their disposal. Often, it meant walking miles through the snow-covered woods from Central or Copper Falls.

There are no records available to show names of all the faithful laity that assisted the priests in maintaining the buildings and grounds; cooking; house cleaning; caring for the altar linens and flowers; ushers; choirs; organists; opening and closing the church daily for summer visitors; acolytes; lectors; Eucharist ministers; sextons and many other chores. For those acts of love and charity, I pray they will receive their thanks upon "arrival at the eternal shore."

Robert F. Carlton
Eagle Harbor, Michigan
May 2004

Preface

Many books, periodicals, organizations, and associations have recorded the extraordinary life and accomplishments of Bishop Frederic Baraga.

One of his many accomplishments was serving the spiritual needs of white settlers that were colonizing the Lake Superior Copper District in the mid-19th century.

Frederic Baraga was born 29 June 1797 in the Duchy of Carniola, province of Slovenia, all part of the Austrian Empire; Carniola had been a part of the Holy Roman Empire of Charlemagne since the year 800. Succeeding Holy Roman emperors initiated a program of colonization of their borders with many farmers, former knights and craftsmen and sent them to the thinly populated frontier to spread the Catholic faith. Carniola was the recipient of this early missionary work and Frederic Baraga would ultimately continue the missionary tradition of his forefathers in the new world that became the United States.

In the 1600's explorer and fur trader Pierre Radisson traveled and mapped a route along Lake Superior whose primary purpose was commercial. At about the same period two Catholic missionaries, Rene Menard, and Claude Allouez, from the Society of Jesus (Jesuits); traveled the same route, although their goal was to evangelize the Native American Indians who resided in the vicinity.

As Jesuit missionary activities dwindled, it was about 200 years before any Catholic mission work reappeared on the **"POINT"; the point of land extending out into Lake Superior from the "Kewauenau." Kewauenau-Ojibwa for *place where we cross by land carrying a canoe."***

In Baraga's early years of education at Ljubljana, German and Latin were compulsory studies since most of the textbooks were printed in those languages, very few in his native Slovene. After Napoleon's army invaded and occupied that part of the Austrian Empire, French was made compulsory, and the Slovene language was also encouraged as a mark of good will by the French occupiers.

His education continued as he went on to spend five years in law school in Vienna. While in Law School he studied English, Spanish, and French plus taking advance courses in German and Italian.

Early on in his University of Vienna law school studies, he was attracted to the inspiring Redemptorist priest who lived near the university, Father Clement Hofbauer. In 1808 Hofbauer had been banned from Warsaw, after Napoleon's occupation of Poland, for his zealous Catholic mission work there.

There was a wave of anti-clerical sentiment throughout Austria and other parts of Europe at the time, however the Archbishop of Vienna appointed Father Hofbauer confessor to the Ursuline nuns and director of their church. The duties of Father Hofbauer consisted of hearing the sisters' confessions and spiritual director of their convent church, Saint Ursula's; for this he received free use of an apartment across the street from the convent and a modest salary.

Between 1813-1820 the apartment became a special kind of cloister, a private chapel, a meeting place for famous personalities, a confessional, an assembly room for panel discussions (which included Baraga) and a place where missionary excellence would radiate. Father Hofbauer died in his apartment at the striking of the Angelus on the morning of 15 March 1820. Baraga's association with Father Hofbauer led the young student to give up his plan to remain in the field of law after graduation and consider the priesthood.

In 1821 Baraga graduated from Law School with excellent grades, then returned home where he gave up his claim to the family castle at TREBNJE and informed his intended future bride that he was going to become a priest. On All SAINTS DAY 1 November 1821, he entered the seminary of Laibach, and he was ordained at the Cathedral of Saint Nicolas in Ljubljana, Slovenia on 21 September 1823.

In 1827, Bishop Edward Fenwick of the diocese of Cincinnati, which covered the state of Ohio and the territories of Michigan and Wisconsin, pleaded with European sources to send missionary priests willing to help him fulfill the spiritual needs of the rapidly growing immigrant population plus the thousands of Native Americans in his diocese.

Father Baraga was one of those answering the call and on 30 December 1830 landed in New York. With the zeal of Father Clement Hofbauer[1], who had a profound influence on him, Father Baraga, the new missionary, started his crusade to serve the Native American Indians.

---

[1] Father Clement Maria Hofbauer of the congregation of the Most Holy Redeemer (Redemptorist) was proclaimed venerable in 1888, by Pope Leo XII and in 1909, Pius X declared Clement a saint and made him patron Saint of Vienna in 1914.

The Church of the Most Holy Redeemer
Eagle Harbor, Michigan

Baraga's Arrival

After arriving in America, Father Baraga's first Indian mission (1831-1833) was with the Ottawa, who inhabited the vicinity of what is now Harbor Springs, Michigan. Between 1833-1835 he established a new mission at what is now Grand Rapids, Michigan. He was successful in baptizing many of his new flock at these two missions, however his goal was to be with the inhabitants living around Lake Superior where there had not been a Catholic missionary since the Jesuits departed in the mid-1600's.

The Lake Superior location he chose was LaPointe, where he built his first missionary church for the Chippewa / Ojibwa. LaPointe is located on one of the Apostle Islands [Madeline Island, near Bayfield, Wisconsin-Ed.], about 300 miles west of Sault Ste. Marie and was an active trading center for Indians and fur traders. Father Baraga was the first Catholic priest to set foot on the island in one hundred sixty-four years. Shortly after arriving, he built a small log church dedicated to Saint Joseph; in 1838 he built a new and larger one to accommodate the growing number of converts. After serving there for eight years, a fur trader invited him to establish a mission amongst the Indian settlement at L'Anse, about one hundred eighty miles to the east of LaPointe. Jesuit Father Rene Menard had established a temporary mission there in 1660 but no permanent priest was assigned to continue his work; therefore, little or no sign of Christianity remained amongst those residing there. In 1844 Father Baraga now made this his permanent center of operations and built a church there he dedicated to the Most Holy Name of Jesus.[2]

---

[2] During the same period, Fort Wilkins was established on the "Point" (Keweenaw peninsula) to protect the influx of immigrants seeking employment related to the discovery of copper.

In the fall of 1846 Father Baraga returned from a trip to Detroit on a ship that stopped at Copper Harbor, which was the closest main port to L'Anse. A raging storm caused him to lay-over there for 10 days which gave him an opportunity to visit Catholics in the area. When the weather cleared, he and his Indian companions departed for L'Anse in canoes with the books and supplies he had brought from Detroit.

In January 1847 he headed north from L'Anse on snowshoes through the forest, some 80 miles, to the mining district (near Copper Harbor) which was rapidly becoming alive with activity. There he found numbers of Irish, German and French-Canadian Catholics busily engaged in exploration for copper. He said Mass for "non-natives" for the first time this side of Sault Ste. Marie at a log house belonging to the Copper Falls Mining Company and occupied by John (Kerry)[3] Carey. Later Mr. (Kerry) Carey built a new home in Eagle River, where Father Baraga said Mass in May 1847. Father Baraga was often a guest of the (Kerry) Carey's hospitality and after becoming Bishop he frequently stayed with them on later trips to the "Point."

During the May 1847 visit he remained in the district for three weeks traveling to various mine locations; Copper Harbor, Eagle River and Eagle Harbor, which were growing communities inhabited by the recent settlers.

In 1852 he said Mass in the Foley-Smith house at Eagle Harbor. Mary Clare Smith resided in the two-family house most of her life (1889-1983); she wrote a letter to Joseph Gregorich in 1955, passing down information gathered from her grandparents, which in part said: *"Father Baraga said mass at one end of the living room and ate his frugal meals prepared by Grandmother (Smith-Ed.) in the other end of the small room and slept in the massive walnut bed upstairs."*

---

[3] Msgr. Rezek in "History of the Diocese of Sault Ste. Marie and Marquette" refers to the phonetic spelling as KERRY; however, Keweenaw County records and family documents show the spelling as CAREY

Mary Claire Smith had been Post Mistress at Eagle Harbor for years, even though she was stone deaf from infancy, she conducted postal business by reading lips. Claire was the daughter of Judge William E. Smith (Keweenaw County Judge of Probate for 40 consecutive years) and Mary Ellen Carey of Eagle River, a daughter of John Carey.

There were no priests available to serve the growing number of Catholics in the mining communities except Father Baraga who made the Indian Mission in L'Anse his headquarters. He established a regular route amongst the numerous mining communities from Copper Harbor to Cliff and attempted visiting them at least twice a year, or more often in case of necessity. This routine was followed until 1853 when he became bishop.

Vicariate Apostolic

On 29 July 1853 the Upper Peninsula of Michigan was detached from the Diocese of Detroit and made a Vicariate Apostolic. The appointed Vicar Apostolic is not always made bishop, but in this instance at the special request of the Fathers of the Plenary Council, which was held in Baltimore in 1852, Baraga was invested with the character of a bishop and as was customary at that time, was given an extinct diocese. On the feast of All Saints Day, 1 November 1853, Frederic Baraga was consecrated Bishop of Amyzonia and Vicar Apostolic of Upper Michigan at the hands of Archbishop Purcell in Cincinnati. Other events re: Bishop Baraga:

On 9 January 1857 Appointed, Bishop of Sault Ste. Marie.

On 23 October 1865 Appointed, Bishop of Sault Ste. Marie-Marquette

Died 19 January 1868 at the age of 70+.

The influx of Catholics arriving from Europe to the mining districts, required more and more priests to serve the rapidly growing population. In early 1854 Bishop Baraga traveled to Europe to recruit seminarians who were preparing for missions abroad and to raise funds for his Vicariate.

At St. Suplice in Paris, a college preparing men for foreign assignments, he found two young men who offered their services, but both had been trained for the missions in INDIA, reluctantly he turned them down realizing some bishop in that country was awaiting their arrival. In his travels to other parts of Europe, he did manage to recruit several others for mission work in the Upper Peninsula.

Building Holy Redeemer at Eagle Harbor

Bishop Baraga selected Eagle Harbor to establish his church because of its central location to the residents of the surrounding mining locations.

On 1 September 1853 the Eagle Harbor Mining Co. conveyed Lots 167 and 168 of Block 22, to Frederic Baraga for the consideration of sixty dollars.

In 1854 lot 166, Block 22 was purchased for one hundred dollars from Dennis Duggan. A contract was given to Nick Grasser to build the church and before winter set in that year it was enclosed and ready for services.

This was the first non-Native American Catholic church built in the Upper Peninsula; Bishop Baraga dedicated it to our "Most Holy Redeemer." Father Clement Hofbauer of the Redemptorist Order (Congregation of the Most Holy Redeemer) had a lasting influence on Baraga's missionary life.

Presently the church property still consists of same three lots: 166, 167, 168 of Block 22 as shown on the map of Eagle Harbor Village.

Anton Grewe of Eagle River donated sixty-five dollars for the bell, which is still in use during the summer season and is rung prior to the celebration of Mass.

Like many churches of that period, it was a combination church and priest residence. The second floor, above the sacristy, consisted of two rooms with a masonry chimney that served heating and cooking stoves for the sparse living quarters. The sanctuary was

2 Interior of church prior to 1900
PHOTO CREDIT: Msgr. Rezek's
"History of the Diocese of Sault Ste. Marie and Marquette - 1906"

heated by a barrel type stove with a stovepipe that off-set through the ceiling near the center of the church. This also radiated heat to those in attendance.

Candles with a metal reflector adorned the walls between the stations-of-the-cross; and a unique confessional/pulpit was built on the east side of the sanctuary. The confessional is located under the pulpit.

Box pews, provided with doors, served to minimize drafts and also maintain some heat for the occupants, who brought heated rocks or bricks with them during the cold months. Several front pews, located on the west side of the sanctuary, had no doors installed to accommodate those serving as pallbearers during funeral services. Box pews were quite common in churches located in the colder climates of the eastern United States that were built during the same era as Holy Redeemer.

First Resident Pastor-Fr. Thiele

Reverend Henry L. Thiele was the first priest ordained in and for the diocese by Bishop Baraga and he was assigned to Eagle Harbor. He was born in 1819 in the province of Hanover, Germany in 1854, he came to America that same year at the invitation of the new bishop and was ordained on 21 October 1854 by Bishop Baraga. He served at Eagle Harbor, (except for a nine-month absence between November 1856 and July 1857), until June 1861. While back at Holy Redeemer; in 1858, he had the church at Cliff mine built, which was later moved to Phoenix. In 1861 he was transferred to Mackinac Island and was so unsatisfied there that the Bishop agreed to his request, and returned him to Eagle Harbor in September of that same year.

In October 1862 he withdrew from the diocese with the intention of joining a religious Order, however, he returned in August 1864, and was made pastor in Marquette. He anticipated the See would be moved to a more central location than Sault Ste. Marie and felt it would be Marquette. Based on this inclination, he commenced building a spacious church in Marquette which later became the first Cathedral. There is a letter on file at Notre Dame Archives, dated 7 September 1866, from Bishop Baraga to Archbishop Purcell asking permission for Father Thiele to put on a fair in Cincinnati for the purpose of raising money to pay the $6,000.00 he still owed on the church at Marquette.

3 Father Thiele
PHOTO CREDIT: Msgr. Rezek's
"History of the Diocese of Sault Ste. Marie
and Marquette - 1906"

His former interest in joining an Order was revived. He resigned his position to spend his declining years with a life-long friend, the Very Rev. Father Sorin, founder of Notre Dame University in South Bend, Indiana. He died there 17 August 1873.

Fr. Jacker's Activities

Very Reverend Edward Jacker. Father Jacker was born 2 September 1827 in Ellwangen, Wuertemberg, Germany and was a significant contributor to the expanding Catholic communities being established in the Copper Country. He was ordained at the Sault 5 August 1855, the second priest ordained by Bishop Baraga for the new diocese. He was sent to L'Anse (Assinins) to work with the Indians. During Father Thiele's absence from Eagle Harbor between November 1856 and July 1857, Father Jacker served both L'Anse and Holy Redeemer at Eagle Harbor.

In April 1860, Father Jacker received, in addition to L'Anse, St. Ignatius in Houghton. The great distance between the two made it impossible to serve both locations on Sunday so he served each, every other week until April 1861 when he was relieved of his duty at L'Anse and moved to Houghton.

In August 1861 St. Anne's church in Hancock was dedicated and he held services in both churches every Sunday. He found it more convenient to live in Hancock and moved there right after dedication of St. Anne's.

In October 1866, Bishop Baraga attended the Second Plenary Council outside the diocese, and he appointed Father Jacker Administrator of the diocese during his absence. Bishop Baraga returned from the Council very ill and from that time until

4 Father Jacker
PHOTO CREDIT: Msgr. Rezek's
"History of the Diocese of Sault Ste. Marie
and Marquette - 1906"

the Bishop's death on 19 January 1868, Father Jacker remained in charge of the diocese until the arrival of Bishop Mrak.

Relieved of his duties in Marquette, Father Jacker went to Calumet to organize a new parish there, Sacred Heart. His first recorded baptism there is 18 April 1868. He remained in Calumet until October 1873 and in November 1873 was assigned to St. Ignace.

Father Jacker was now in charge of the parishes on Mackinaw Island and St. Ignace and became interested in early missionary history. He read and studied historical information related to the subject, plus inquired from old Indians about traditions he knew existed amongst them. Following-up on these sources, one confirming another, his investigations finally led to an ancient site of the early Jesuit chapel and the grave of Father Jacques Marquette (1636-1675), which had been there since about 1677 and forgotten for almost two hundred years.

In 1675 Fr. Marquette after accompanying Joliet on an earlier discovery expedition of the Mississippi River, in what is now Illinois and Wisconsin, returned.

to the area to set up a mission amongst the Illinois Indians. He became very ill from a bout with dysentery that had lingered, from the earlier expedition, which sapped his health. He realized he was too sick to proceed and requested his companions to get him back to St. Ignace. He died at age thirty-nine on the trip up Lake Michigan and was buried on a high riverbank near what is now Ludington, Michigan. The two boatmen companions, then brought his diary and a few of his possessions to the Jesuit mission in St. Ignace.

In l677, an Indian hunting party on the shore of Lake Michigan found the cross that marked his grave, which included his prayer book and rosary. Some of them had been instructed in the Faith by Father Marquette while he was amongst them and he had left a significant impression on them, they decided to return the remains to his countrymen in St. Ignace. The body was disinterred, the bones cleaned in accordance with their custom, dried in the sun, packed in a crude birch- bark box; then a large gathering of Indians in a fleet of canoes, accompanied the remains to St. Ignace. The birch-bark casket was brought to the log chapel and lay there covered with a pall for twenty-four hours, a requiem mass was sung, then it was buried beneath the chapel floor.

In 1700 the St. Ignace chapel burned down while Father Engelran, the Jesuit in charge of the mission, was in Montreal working on a peace settlement amongst various Indian tribes. On his return he found the chapel in ruins, he then built a new and larger one at a different location. Father Marquette's remains were left undisturbed at the old site until Father Jacker's research led to their recovery in 1873. Some of these relics are now preserved in the church at St. Ignace and some at Marquette University in Milwaukee.

Father Jacker was recalled from St. Ignace and returned to Marquette where he again became administrator of the diocese until Bishop Vertin arrived; he was then sent to Hancock as pastor of St. Anne's. In July 1884 he resigned his pastorate to retire at Holy Redeemer, Eagle Harbor where he could devote more time to studies and writing. Eagle Harbor was still bustling with mission activities required by the many Catholics in the mining locations at Delaware, Central, Copper Falls, Eagle River and Copper Harbor which precluded him from devoting much time to his retirement goals. At his own request he was sent to Detour where the routine was much slower. He died in Marquette on 1 September 1887 and is buried in Hancock. Father Jacker's tomb stone is located at the foot of the bell tower on the grounds of the Church of the Resurrection in Hancock; also, a street near Saint Ignatius Loyola church in Houghton is named Jacker Street. Jacker Street is located one block south of Baraga Avenue; during their lifetime, Bishop Baraga and Father Jacker had been close and loyal friends.

Fr. Andolshek

Father Andrew Jacob Andolshek was born in Reifhitz, Carniola (present-day Slovenia-Ed.), 27 September 1827 and served at Eagle Harbor on two different occasions. He served there from April until September 1861, he then returned to serve there from November 1879 until his death from acute consumption 23 June 1882. He is buried in the Eagle Harbor cemetery, his remains resting in a north-south direction. The burial plot was located adjacent to a large wooden cross that no longer exists.

Priests that were assigned to Eagle Harbor from 1854-1895 and the Keweenaw Missions from 1905 through the present, are listed in chronological order in Appendix I.

Resident priests were assigned to Holy Redeemer from 1854 until the decline of the copper mines in northern Keweenaw County, about 1895.

For the next ten years priests from parishes in Calumet and Lake Linden paid occasional visits to Eagle Harbor until 1905.

The Franciscan Fathers (St. John the Baptist Province, Cincinnati, Ohio) provided priests to the Keweenaw Missions from 1905-1963 and 1978-2001.

On 6 August 1963 Father John McCardle was appointed to the newly created responsibility of Administrator of St. Mary's Parish, Mohawk as resident pastor which included all of Keweenaw County. Diocesan priests were assigned until 1978.

In 1978 the Keweenaw Missions were again the responsibility of the Franciscan's with the assignment of Father Faron Boyle, O.F.M. The Franciscans remained until their departure in 2001.

From 2001 until the present, the dioceses provide a priest from St. Paul the Apostle in Calumet, Father Sebastian Ettolil, MCBS (Missionary Congregation of the Blessed Sacrament). In addition to St. Paul's, he is responsible for year-round Mass at Our Lady of Peace, Ahmeek and summer services at Holy Redeemer plus Our Lady of the Pines, Copper Harbor.

Rectory

In 1884, Father Jacker returned to Eagle Harbor planning to study and write in the solitude this remote locale offered. One of his first projects was to build a small rectory behind the church that would improve the resident priest's living conditions. It had been thirty years since Father Jacker had served at Holy Redeemer and he was aware what the sparse quarters above the church offered.

St Joseph's church, which was located in the town of Wyoming, adjacent to the

5 Rectory circa 1900
PHOTO CREDIT: Msgr. Rezek's
"History of the Diocese of Sault Ste. Marie and Marquette - 1906"

Delaware mine, was a mission of Holy Redeemer. In 1892 production at the mine was declining and families were leaving to seek employment elsewhere. The church was closed and Father Nosbisch, made use of lumber and building materials from St Joseph's to enlarge the rectory at Holy Redeemer, an add-on to that which Father Jacker had built in 1884. Mrs. Frances Rozich has an itemized inventory of items sent from St. Joseph's to Holy Redeemer, which include artificial flowers, vases, bed

6 Rectory 2003
PHOTO CREDIT: Bob Masnado

sheets, pillows, framed pictures, etc. and signed by Father Nosbisch in 1892.

The rectory was again enlarged by Father Juniper Hukenbeck, OFM, who cared for Holy Redeemer from 1934-1944. Presently, the old building has electricity, indoor plumbing, and several other improvements have taken place since Father Jacker's first phase was completed one hundred nineteen years ago.

Father Ed. Lammert OFM, a former Buckeye Boy, has been vacationing at the Holy Redeemer rectory every summer since 1962, he has surveyed the building and found some large beams (14"x14") under the floor, the type used by mining companies and thought to have originally come from St, Joseph's in Delaware.

Presently, the water is drained from the house in the fall, then is reopened prior to the first Mass in June. The church and rectory are cleaned by volunteers. For years Keweenaw Missions parishioners from Mohawk, Ahmeek and Copper City came equipped with cleaning items to have both buildings ready for the summer activities. After the cleaning tasks were completed, the volunteers retired to the rectory for a picnic lunch, conversation, and a joyful songfest.

In recent years, several retirees now reside in or near Eagle Harbor; many of them volunteer and participate in the spring-cleaning chores plus maintaining the buildings and grounds.

Currently, the rectory shows signs of old age and requires much needed maintenance to preserve its historical value.

Cemetery

Historically, burial places were often in private ownership and confined to isolated plots of ground which evolved into areas of the Christian community in common.

Old customs played a large part in dealing with the dead and where their bodies were laid to rest. When a burial ground was not in the church yard, it was usually located at a reasonable distance from the church for pallbearers to carry the remains to the burial site. At Eagle Harbor the pallbearers carried the casket to the cemetery on a funeral bier which was hand carved and fabricated from saplings that grew in the area. The body was then laid to rest in the confines of the designated burial plot with the feet facing east.

Customarily, a conspicuous large and well-built cross was erected in the area signifying consecrated ground and a wall or other boundary, sufficient to keep out stray animals, that encompassed the entire property. When there was no wall or fence installed, the deceased's family often installed a private enclosure or fence to add some privacy to the loved one's resting spot. These privacy plots are conspicuous in the Eagle Harbor cemetery, probably dating back to a period prior to a perimeter fence being installed.

7 Handmade Funeral Bier
PHOTO CREDIT: Bob Carlton

In Richard Jilbert's census of Pine Grove Cemetery there are notations of burials dated in 1852 and 1853; however, it was not until November 1866 that Eagle Harbor Copper Company deeded the Township five acres in section Six (Vol. F 229) to be used as a burial ground.

At the annual meeting of the Township electors held on 2 April 1877, they voted to execute a deed of the Catholic Burial ground at Eagle Harbor and convey it to Bishop Mrak of Marquette and his successor.

On 10 July 1877 Eagle Harbor Township conveyed a deed (Vol.G 559) to Bishop Mrak and successors with boundaries described for the NW Quarter of Section Six containing five acres, more or less.

From 1877 until 1966 this portion of the cemetery was considered to be the Catholic Cemetery; however, in 1966 the validity of the property at issue was questioned with the following conclusion: A letter on file at the Keweenaw Missions, dated 19 January 1966, in part says:

At the time the Township conveyed the Eagle Harbor Cemetery to Bishop Mrak of Marquette, there was a specific Michigan statute in which the township was required to follow to convey the township interest in the cemetery. Section One (l), Act Two Hundred Fifteen (215) of 1861 part of which reads:

> **"No real estate shall be sold by the virtue of this act which is or has been in actual use as or on burial grounds, unless the same is be sold by an Order of the Circuit Court upon Petition of the Board of Health of the township in which the cemetery ground is situated."**

The County Clerk researched the records to see if any of the above requirements of the 1861 Act could be located and found none. The conclusion was, at the time of the transfer to the Bishop of Marquette in1866, the Township Board was not in compliance with the 1861 statute, therefore Eagle Harbor Township remains owner of the property.

8 Old Catholic Cemetery
Eagle Harbor (1877-1966)
PHOTO CREDIT: Mrs. Frances Rozich

The first death appearing in the Holy Redeemer Church record book is:

John Quinza — age 37
died 28 January 1855 at North American Mine
Son of Anton and Maria Quinza S/ Fr. H. L. Thiele

No burial site is recorded; however, the North American Mine was located on top the bluff, near the Cliff Mine.

In September 1882 Father Andolshek died of consumption while serving as pastor of Holy Redeemer and is buried in what was the Catholic Cemetery. His remains were laid to rest in a north-south direction while it is customary to bury remains with the feet pointing east. The grave is marked with a metal monument mounted on a concrete base that was located at the foot of large wooden cross. The base was crumbling and disintegrating from years of exposure to the environment such that the metal monument was on the verge of toppling.

9 Father Anolshek's Grave (*Before*)
PHOTO CREDIT: Msgr. Rezek's
"History of the Diocese of Sault Ste. Marie
and Marquette - 1906"

During the summer of 2003, Robert (Buzz) Johnson Contracting was doing repairs on Holy Redeemer Church, he donated material and labor to rebuild the base and remount the monument. The old large wooden cross has been removed, the burial area has been recently surveyed by James Heikkila of Mohawk, Richard Jilbert of Eagle Harbor has developed a computerized list of known burials and a sexton has been appointed to oversee cemetery activities. The burial ground is known as Pine Grove Cemetery of Eagle Harbor

Delaware

In 1863 Bishop Baraga purchased Lots 1 and 2 of Block 3 in the Village of Wyoming, Township of Eagle Harbor, from the Pennsylvania Mining Company of Michigan, with the intention of building a church on the site. At that time, the nearby Delaware mine was active and there were numerous families residing in the vicinity. Father P. M. Flannigan, pastor at Eagle Harbor, built the church and rectory on the south side of the Montreal River in what was called Hill-town; the town took on a local

10 Father Anolshek's Grave (*2004*)
PHOTO CREDIT: Bob Carlton

identification and was nicknamed "hell-town" because of its many saloon brawls and fights. Services were held in the new church immediately upon completion, however it remained undedicated for almost seven years until the 1870's when it was named for Saint Joseph. With the closing of the mines the church was no longer needed and lumber from the rectory was used in the 1892 rectory extension at Eagle Harbor. What remained of the church was destroyed by vandals.

Phoenix-Cliff

In the summer of 1865. Bishop Baraga appointed Father Mathias Orth resident pastor to Saint Mary's Church at Cliff, to minimize travel for the priest residing at Eagle Harbor. A year later the Cliff Mine was waning, and the population dwindled; therefore, the church no longer required a permanent resident pastor.

In 1899 the Phoenix Consolidated

11 St. Joseph's Church Wyoming (Delaware), circa 1890
PHOTO CREDIT: Msgr. Rezek's "History of the Diocese of Sault Ste. Marie and Marquette - 1906"

Copper Company was formed by what had been old Phoenix, St.Clair, and the Garden City mines which increased the population in the vicinity. To provide a place of worship, Father Smietana had the old Cliff church moved to Phoenix and re-erected upon the site it rests today, which was donated by the mining company. The economy of Phoenix all but disappeared as the mines closed and the residents moved on.

Prior to its closing as an active church, Mass was conducted periodically during the summer months by the Franciscan's as part of the Keweenaw Catholic Missions. In 1946 Joseph Thieler and Cecilia Negro were one of the last couples to be married there at this church. The old church showed signs of long-term neglect and prior to his wedding, Joe Thieler, a local lumberman, had the church repainted and the church steps rebuilt, with the assistance of Peter Negro.

It is now maintained by the Keweenaw County Historical Society.

Central

At Central Mine, for thirty years the company permitted Catholics the use of a building which burned down in 1903. Subsequently, they were given permission to use an empty house across the street from where the church stood. An altar was brought from the old Cliff church and with a few alterations the new site served as a chapel for Mass.

On 9 October1904 a heavy wind blew the building off its supports where it rested on the ground. Mr. Peter Schuler was custodian of these properties for years and his granddaughter Mrs. Frances (Schuler) Rozich of Mohawk provided the information below.

Schuler Memories

12 Chapel at Central prior to 1906
PHOTO CREDIT: Msgr. Rezek's
"History of the Diocese of Sault Ste. Marie and Marquette - 1906"

Peter Schuler

Peter Schuler came to this country from Germany at age 18, landing at Eagle Harbor.

From there he went to Northwestern Mine, where he worked for a short time, and then left for Detroit. Not liking it in Detroit he soon returned to the Northwestern Mine and stayed there until the Central Mine opened. When the Central Mine started operations in 1854, he became one of its first employees. He worked for a short time underground and then became employed on surface at the rock house. In later years he became foreman on surface and when the mine closed in 1898, he remained as caretaker of the property until his death in 1916.

Louisa Kampf left her native Germany a few years later (than Peter-Ed.) landed at Eagle Harbor and then came to Central where she was employed by Mr. Petrie, the mine agent, as a hired girl.

It was here she met Peter Schuler and they were married at Eagle Harbor on 15 September 1861, by Father Andrew Andolshek. To this union eight children were born, one of who is still living today (1964-Ed.), John, who supplied the information for this story:

"In our early years we attended church at Eagle Harbor or Cliff Mine. I can recall going to Mass at Delaware. If for any reason, we could not attend Mass on Sunday we were required to pray the Mass at home from our Missal.

Beginning in the (18) seventies Mass was said at Central Mine in a building donated for this purpose by the mining company. The priest residing in Eagle Harbor took care of the Mission at Central. Masses were said at 8:30 and 10:30 alternately between the two towns.

When the early Mass was at Central the priest would walk up on Saturday, unless given a ride, and stayed at the Schuler home overnight. After the 8:30 Mass one of the parishioners would have a horse ready waiting to take the priest back to Eagle Harbor for the second Mass. This was a distance of five miles so there was no time lost in keeping this schedule.**

Likewise, when the 8:30 Mass was at Eagle Harbor, someone from there drove the priest up to Central after the first Mass.

13 Peter Schuler
PHOTO CREDIT: Msgr. Rezek's
"History of the Diocese of Sault Ste. Marie and Marquette - 1906"

After the second Mass the priest was invited to the Schuler home for breakfast and often spent several hours visiting the family. Later in the day one of the boys drove him back to the Harbor.

I very distinctly remember making my first Communion and being confirmed on the same day by Bishop Vertin at Eagle Harbor in the year 1890. Previous to that we received instructions from Father Schelhammer for one week. During this week we boarded at the Elias home at Eagle Harbor and attended instructions all day, every day of the week. Our evenings were free, and it was a treat for us boys to go fishing in the strange creeks about the Harbor.

I also remember that during the Mass and Confirmation, Miss Anne Conners played the organ and sang. There never was an organ or singing at the Central church.

I also remember one year my father hired a team and our whole family went to Eagle Harbor to Midnight Mass.

Miss Mary Skulley was housekeeper for Father Schelhammer at Eagle Harbor. Father Jacker's brother, William, kept house for him, also at Eagle Harbor.

When the Cliff church moved to Phoenix, we went to Mass there. Father Smietana was the first pastor of the Phoenix church. His sister kept house for him at the rear of the church.
We continued to attend Mass at the Phoenix church until 1922, when we moved to Mohawk, where I have attended St. Mary's since."

As told to me by my father, John Schuler, age 86, 2 February 1964.

By: Frances S. Rozich

Foley Memories

Paul Foley of Mohawk described some stories his father (Michael) had shared with him about growing up in Eagle Harbor.

Michael Foley was born at Eagle Harbor in 1881 and resided there until he was 21. As a boy Michael and his brother George served as altar boys at Holy Redeemer in the late 1880's and early 1890's. Michael had vivid memories of Christmas eves he carried through his entire life. Parishioners decorated the church with pine boughs that were fastened to the "stations of the cross" and reflective candles mounted on the walls illuminated the church. The barrel stove in front of the pews produced much needed heat and the smell of fresh pine filled the church. It was amazing to see families from Central and Copper Falls walking down the hill in single file along the snow-covered path then over to the church which they filled to capacity.

Sunday Vespers and May Devotions were held at church and parents saw to it that youth attendance was compulsory.

As the local mines declined, the surrounding population dwindled as well as church activities.

The Foley brothers moved to Mohawk and opened a meat market there in the year 1902.

Paul Foley was one of several acolytes from St. Mary's, Mohawk or Sacred Heart, Calumet that accompanied the Franciscans on their visits to say Mass at Eagle Harbor or Phoenix, during the 1920's and 1930's.

Saint Mary's - Calumet

Father Anthony Molinari served at Holy Redeemer in 1892 and 1893. Msgr. Rezek's history describes the circumstance of Father Molinari being at Eagle Harbor as follows:

The Calumet area Italians were served by Sacred Heart Church and as other nationalities were erecting their own churches the Italians planned the same.

Bishop Vertin sent Father Anthony Molinari to assist their effort. Father Molinari succeeded in raising a large sum of money in a few months for the building that was scheduled to start in the upcoming spring. A labor dispute broke out amongst the miners and C&H, in which some Italians and others participated. During the work stoppage an accident at Whiting Shaft occurred (which cost the lives often men), on a Sunday which was also the Feast of the Blessed Virgin. The Italians and Austrians requested they not be forced to work that day, C&H refused their request and the Italians "walked out." C&H then refused to give any property for the intended church. The church project was dropped, the money collected was returned and Father Molinari was sent to Eagle Harbor.

As C&H and the Italians settled their differences; C&H continued with its practice, as with other nationalities and gave the usual support of two-thousand dollars ($2000.00) in cash and two lots fronting on Portland Street. Father Molinari returned to the project in August 1897, Bishop Vertin dedicated Saint Mary's church 12 October 1897; the church the Italians built then became a 350-family parish.

Population Shift

The closing of mines in the surrounding area caused the local economy to falter and a population exodus from Eagle Harbor. Between 1895-1898 only occasional Mass was offered at the church until a regular pastor could be assigned; between 1898-1904 various short-term pastors held the position.

Mining operations had shifted to southern Keweenaw County and the northern portions of Houghton County as did the center of population.

During this period there was little, or no maintenance accomplished on the church or rectory.

The last regularly assigned pastor to Holy Redeemer was Father A. Deschamps, 30 August 1903 - 12 June 1904. It had been fifty-years since Bishop Baraga sent Father Thiele to administer the sacraments to the influx of white settlers in northern Keweenaw County. Beginning in 1905 through 1963 the Franciscan

14 Neglected church, circa 1903
PHOTO CREDIT: Msgr. Rezek's
"History of the Diocese of Sault Ste. Marie and Marquette - 1906"

Fathers became responsible for Holy Redeemer, which then became a mission of Sacred Heart Church, Calumet.

Catholic Population - 1907

A significant change in the Catholic population had taken place since 1854 when Bishop Baraga chose Eagle Harbor to be the center for his mission church. In the span of 53 years the dynamics of the mining activities shifted the economics of the Copper Country.

A 26 November 1907 article in the Calumet News offered some population statistics as follows:

It has been ascertained, as accurately as it is possible to learn by means of a thorough census, that there are 27,238 persons in Houghton County who pledge their allegiance to the Roman Catholic Church. Of these by far the greater numbers are found in Calumet and the immediate vicinity. According to the census enumeration just completed by the Catholic priests, Calumet has a Catholic population of 13,141.

There are no less than six Catholic churches in Calumet. The Sacred Heart at Hecla has in its parish, according to the enumeration of Father Casmir, 1700 people; St. Anthony's, which is largely attended by the Polish residents of Calumet, has a membership of 1259, and the St. Joseph church, Slovenian, (now St. Paul the Apostle-Ed.), has probably the largest number in its parish of any in the copper country. It has been found to lack only fifty of being 3000.

St. Anne's church (French-Ed.) has 2,032 communicants and St. Mary's (Italian-Ed.), 2800. The Croatian church, St. John de Baptiste, has a membership of 2400.

Franciscan Fathers 1905-1963

The Franciscan Fathers were responsible for Holy Redeemer on two separate occasions. The province of Saint John the Baptist, Cincinnati, Ohio provided priests for Sacred Heart parish in Calumet from 1880-2001; Sacred Heart then provided Friar Pastors to the Keweenaw Missions between 1905-1963; then after 15 years of diocesan priests serving the Missions, again the provincial sent Friars to administer the Keweenaw Catholic Missions between 1978-2001.

During the 1920's and 1930's the mission priest from Sacred Heart would circulate from Mohawk to Gay, then during the summer he also would alternate between Eagle Harbor and Phoenix to offer Mass. Altar boys from Mohawk accompanied him on his trek and during the winter the Foley Brothers provided a horse and cutter for transportation to Gay.

The physical condition of the church and rectory at Eagle Harbor had been neglected for several years until the 1930's. The economic depression hit the Copper Country with a vengeance and the mining industry was devastated; unemployment was rampant except for federal government sponsored projects that offered some benefits to the people. Keweenaw County Road Commission put men to work building the Lakeshore Drive, Mountain Drive, Keweenaw Golf Course, plus bringing electric power and a public water system to Eagle Harbor.

15 Holy Redeemer church, circa 1910
House on the right owned by Annie Auger,
great-grandmother of Marilynn Ehrenreich
of Eagle Harbor
PHOTO CREDIT
Michigan Technological University Archives and
Copper Country Historical Collections

Bishop Baraga Society/Association

In 1930 the Bishop Baraga Association was organized in Chicago by Joseph Gregorich (from the Iron Range of Minnesota migrated to Chicago) to promote Baraga's sainthood. He spent his free time collecting letters, works and historical data on Frederic Baraga's priestly life. He and his wife accumulated thousands of items; their Chicago residence was crammed with memorabilia related to Baraga's life in the United States and Europe.

This writer's daughter (Kathleen) was a Librarian in the Des Plaines, IL schools at that time (1976-1977), and a member of the Bishop Baraga Association; through some research she located and visited Mr. and Mrs. Gregorich.

Mr. Gregorich had spent years collecting items he feared would get lost or not be properly accounted for. There were historical items in Marquette that were in storage at various locations and an inventory would be required prior to advancing the Cause in Rome. As a result of the meeting with Mr. Gregorich, Kathleen agreed to donate her services to the Cause, arrange for a sabbatical from the school district, and go to Marquette to inventory and account for items related to Bishop Baraga. In 1977 Bishop Charles Salatka approved the plan and provided her with lodging at the Sisters of St. Paul Convent in Marquette. She spent months gathering material into a central location, taking inventory, and numbering items and arranging for the next step in the cataloging process that was a forerunner to the current well organized Baraga Archives conducted by Elizabeth Delene in Marquette.

Bishop Baraga Day I

In the 1930's, interest in the saintly life of Bishop Baraga brought renewed attention to Holy Redeemer. By June 1934 money was raised to accomplish some maintenance of the building, a new roof was installed, and the interior was repainted.

In August of that summer (1934) the first field Mass was offered in the Eagle Harbor Town Square (present ball field), by Father Bonaventure Kilfoyle, O.F.M., celebrating Bishop Baraga Day. Crowds poured into town to make the outdoor Mass a Memorial Day.

Upkeep

In 1936 the exterior of the church was painted by a group of volunteers from the Keweenaw County Road Commission under the direction of Pat Reagan, who were building the Lakeshore Drive and Mountain Drive between Eagle and Copper Harbor.

In 1938 the sacristy was renovated, and new carpet was laid around the altar in the sanctuary made possible by gifts from George and Hanna Rice of Eagle Harbor (who knew Bishop Baraga) and a donation from the Bishop Baraga Society.

The resurgence in interest in Holy Redeemer brought occasional visiting priest to the rectory during summer vacation periods and in addition to Sundays, daily Mass would be celebrated during their stay.

An event that lives vividly in the memory of this writer took place one cloudy summer day in the mid-1930's during Mass. The organ being used at the time was a manual pump type, manipulated by the organist feet and was located on the main floor just to the left upon entering the church. A kerosene lamp, providing light for the organist, was located on a small shelf attached to the side of the organ. The resulting motion from the pumping action caused the lamp to fall to the floor, the fuel to spill and burst into flames. The usher, who was standing in the rear of the church, took immediate action, tore off his suit coat

16 Carl Beauchamp, driver of the mail wagon
that picked up mail at the Keweenaw Central Depot in Delaware
and delivered to Eagle Harbor post office.
PHOTO CREDIT: Mrs Frances Rozich

and smothered the flames before the old wooden floor could sustain ignition. The usher was Carl Beauchamp an old time Eagle Harbor resident who resided on the corner of South and Third Streets. Without his quick action the ensuing accident could have been a disaster that may have destroyed the building and today the location would be a spot on the map where there was once a historic church. From 1905-1963 the Franciscan Fathers from Sacred Heart, Calumet had served the Keweenaw Missions; Sacred Heart in Ahmeek was a mission of St. John the Baptist, Croatian Church in Calumet the priests were Capuchin Franciscans.

Keweenaw as a Parish 1963-1977

In July 1963 Bishop Noa appointed Father John McArdle, a Marquette diocesan priest, as the first resident priest at St. Mary's, Mohawk, which included the other Keweenaw

County Catholic churches. He was to form a parish.

Upon the arrival of Father McArdle there was a bed on the third floor of St. Mary's that was used by mission priest in case of staying over for some reason,

July 27, 1963

Reverend John F. McArdle
Holy Family Church
Ontonagon, Michigan

Dear Father McArdle:

By the present letter I wish to inform you that you will be appointed as Administrator of St. Mary's Parish, Mohawk, Michigan, a mission of Sacred Heart Parish, Calumet. This constitutes St. Mary's, Mohawk, a parish with a resident pastor, which will include the entire Keweenaw Peninsula.

The duties of this office will be effective on Tuesday, August 6, 1963.

In the meantime, you are instructed to gather information about a residence. Our plan calls for the erection of a residence as well as a church in Mohawk. Temporary arrangements can be made for residence with the Administrator of St. Ann's parish in Calumet, and temporary church facilities might be available at Sacred Heart church, Ahmeek, which is a mission of St. John's, Calumet.

Extra help for the summer months might be available to you with the Franciscan Fathers of Sacred Heart parish in Calumet.

With every good wish for success in your new venture, I am,

Sincerely yours in Christ,

Bishop of Marquette.

REPRINTED WITH PERMISSION
Fr. John McArdle

such as bad weather. A small office was located on the second floor adjoining the confessional, a stove and a toilet were in the basement.

Plans were formulated to rent the four rooms located over the old Keweenaw Savings Bank which was across the street from the church; two rooms had served as a dentist office and the other two had been the Draft Board office. It took several months to renovate the rooms to serve as a rectory until the current rectory was built, subsequently the old Bank was razed.

While Father McArdle was still there (1963-1967) the Franciscan Order (Croatian) gave up St. John's in Calumet and the mission at Sacred Heart, Ahmeek; the Bishop closed St. Joseph's in Gay as a mission; thereafter, the Keweenaw Missions consisted of Holy Redeemer, Eagle Harbor; Our Lady of the Pines, Copper Harbor; Sacred Heart, Ahmeek; and St. Mary's, Mohawk.

With the assignment of a Pastor to the Keweenaw Missions as a parish, there were many administrative and legal details requiring attention that were neglected in the sixty-plus years since the last full-time priest served at Holy Redeemer.

During Father McArdle's tenure the Bishop Baraga artifact display cabinets were constructed and installed at Holy Redeemer by several Mohawk men from St. Mary's, the names of those who participated in the project are enshrined under the Altar Missal Stand in the display cabinet they built. One of the items displayed on

17 Fr. McArdle and St. Mary's Mohawk choir party
at Eagle Harbor May 1965
PHOTO CREDIT: Fr. John McArdle

the wall is a relic of St. Ursula that relates to Baraga's early days with Father Hofbauer in Vienna.

The colored tiles used in the displays located in the back of church are intended to reflect the Eagle Harbor countryside, white and blue for the sky, green for surrounding greenery and brown for the woods.

Father Norman Clisch served the Keweenaw Parish 1970 until the spring of 1972, during his tenure the Mohawk rectory was built. Property for a new church and rectory had been purchased and Bishop Salatka directed the rectory be constructed on a corner of the site so it could be sold without losing all the land that was designated for a new church.

In 1972, the National Park Service, National Register of Historical Places contains the following entry: Holy Redeemer Church (added 1972- Building #72000629) Located off US-41, Eagle Harbor, Michigan

In 1972 Father John Landreville became pastor of the four Keweenaw Mission churches; Masses were offered at Eagle Harbor and Copper Harbor only during the summer months. Occasionally, a visiting priest assisted in the ministry while vacationing and often stayed in the small living quarters in the rear of Our Lady of the Pines, Copper Harbor. To assist the parish financially, a Summer Festival was held at Gabe Chopp Park in Ahmeek. During this period several large tents were purchased to accommodate the numerous activities and large crowds that flocked to enjoy the music, food and games. A former parishioner, who had left the area, returned each year to assist Father Landreville as Chairman of the Festival Committee. While here, he and his family stayed at Eagle Harbor at the Holy Redeemer rectory, which was normally the only usage the old building received. A young man from Mohawk, Gary Saari, assisted Father with the upkeep at Eagle Harbor with grounds-keeping, opening, and closing the church and rectory for the summer season.

In 1977 Father Landreville was assigned to St. Christopher's in Marquette and was the last diocesan priest to serve as pastor of the Keweenaw Catholic Missions.

Franciscan Fathers Return 1978-2001

In 1978 St. John the Baptist's Province, Franciscan Fathers of Cincinnati, again provided priests to administer the Keweenaw Catholic Missions. Father Faran Boyle, O.F.M. became pastor and moved to the Mohawk rectory; in addition to the four Keweenaw churches, the Calumet Air Force Station (Radar Base) was included in his ministry. The Radar Base, near Gratiot Lake, provided a Base Chapel for the military personnel and their families, which consisted of a small Quonset hut. The non-denominational setting was arranged for Catholic Mass, the altar was prepared accordingly, and a small lectern was used as a pulpit. After the Eagle and Copper Harbor churches were closed for the summer season, residents of

18 Peter Clevenstine – Theresa Carlton wedding
performed by Fr. Faran Boyle, OFM
and Rev. Dr. Ralph Jalkanen (seated on left side of the altar)
May 1979
PHOTO CREDIT: Clevenstine's

these locations were welcomed to attend Mass at the Base Chapel, which was a great convenience during the snow-covered winter season

Church Alterations

In 1984, Friar Matthew Krempel, O.F.M. relieved Father Faran Boyle as pastor of Keweenaw Catholic Missions (KCM); he preferred to be addressed as "Friar" Matthew, rather than "Father." Shortly after his arrival he continued the review of the physical status of St. Mary's, Mohawk, Sacred Heart, Ahmeek; and Holy Redeemer which Father Faran had started. In September 1984, he and representatives from Herman Gundlach, Inc., conducted an on-site inspection of those churches to analyze their condition and estimate the cost of repairs. At Holy Redeemer the interior was showing signs of water damage from roof leaks, window frames were in poor condition, the steeple was leaning and no longer plumb, parts of the wooden ceiling were coming loose and required resetting and the foundation required some rework.

In May 1986, master builder Robert (Buzz) Johnson, reviewed the Gundlach Report with Friar Matthew and volunteered his services to prepare a priority list and a cost estimate. He did a survey by crawling under the building to analyze the foundation, up into the interior of the steeple and belfry and the area above the church ceiling. Costs were a significant factor, and the Johnson Report recommended those items that should be given first consideration to maintain

19 Interior prior to Vatican II, circa 1950
PHOTO CREDIT: Mrs. Frances Rozich

structural integrity of the building and stay within the limited budget. All the fixes that Gundlach had suggested, would have gone way beyond the anticipated budget.

In the summer of 1986, Friar Matthew held several meetings at Holy Redeemer gathering local parishioners together to discuss the proposed renovations and finances. There was a heated discussion regarding the building exterior, rework and repaint the old original wood siding or cover it with vinyl siding. Much of the original siding was deteriorating from years of exposure to the weather and replacement to its original condition was preferred, from a historical standpoint, however far too expensive. Friar made the decision to install vinyl over the existing siding. Kate Kanaley, Pat Taylor, Ann Bach and Paul Ryan drafted a letter of appeal that was sent out canvassing for funds to accomplish the necessary repairs; Howard Taylor chaired the money campaign and funds were received by Keweenaw Catholic Missions in Mohawk.

20 Interior after Vatican II
PHOTO CREDIT: Keweenaw Catholic Mission Files

In the fall of 1986, a contract was awarded to B.W. Construction Company, (Robert E. Wales) of Atlantic Mine for about $19,000.00 for specific repairs. Work included repairs to interior of steeple, install a 30-foot support beam under front (south end) of building, replace glass on six main windows, rebuild front exterior entrance stairs, repair front entrance doors, install new asphalt shingles on roof, install new exterior vinyl siding, paint exterior trim and tuck point foundation.

In the spring of 1987 additional contracts were awarded for interior work. The large wooden cross (Mission 1874) was moved to the rear row of pews and is now attached to the choir loft railing.

St. John's Church, located on Washington Street, Marquette had recently been closed and was being dismantled about the time repairs were being done at Holy Redeemer. While conducting business in Marquette, Friar Matthew requested the Diocesan Chancellor for permission to salvage several items from St. John's for use at Eagle Harbor, which included the large Crucifix, which is now installed behind the altar: statues of Blessed Mother and Saint Joseph and a holy water font. Friar had the statues refurbished through a religious goods store in Lower Michigan that contracted a Chicago artist to repaint them.

21 Crucifix from St. John's Marquette
Baldachin (wooden canopy) from
St. Mary's, Mohawk
PHOTO CREDIT: Elizabeth Delene, Archivist

Additional interior work consisted of extending the raised floor area around the altar; dismantled and removed the original altar rail to accommodate the floor extension; installed two sections of altar rail that came from the recently closed St. Joseph's Church in Gay. Installed new carpeting in the sanctuary; patched and painted the church interior including the pews; carpeted the front entrance and runners up to the altar rail.

Dry walled, painted and installed new trim casings in room to be designated the confessional.

In 1988 the "baldachin" (the wooden canopy attached to the ceiling), that came from the recently closed St. Mary's, Mohawk, was installed above the altar and fitted with new canopy lighting.

The Stations of the Cross were placed back on the renovated walls; however, the original candles that lighted the church since it was built, were not replaced.

After the renovations accomplished between 1987 and 1988, no work had been done to the steeple exterior and the cross mounted on the peak, which remained in a bent position. A crane, equipped with a tall boom, was hired and men went aloft to straighten and re-anchor the cross, plus cover the entire spire with a weather resistant aluminum coating. Prior to recoating, the workers patched over 100 small caliber bullet holes around the steeples surface; it appears the tall silhouette had been a favorite target of some shooter(s) for a good number of years.

The steeple also serves as a beacon for boaters fishing along the Lake Superior coast. Prior to sophisticated electronic fish finders, boaters exiting Eagle Harbor and heading west along the rocky shore used the steeple as a handy landmark. The steeple, which is visible above the treetops, is used as a guide to productive offshore fishing waters. Government navigation charts also show the steeple as a "landmark" for pilots and seafarers.

Father Tom Schmied O.F.M. Capuchin, moved to the Ahmeek area in 1988 as one of the two Capuchins serving in the Diocese of Marquette. He is not assigned to any one parish but does mission work throughout the Upper Peninsula, traveling in his pickup truck, substituting for priest temporarily away from their parish.

In 1988 Friar Matthew was on a mission in Mexico, Father Tom cared for the Keweenaw Catholic Missions until a replacement arrived. During that summer, Father Tom not only attended to the Mass schedule at three churches, while at Eagle Harbor he cleared trees and brush and took care of the yard around the church and rectory.

During this period one of the ladies who had cared for the church linens for years (Mrs. George [Gertrude] Lamerand) passed away and was to be buried from Holy Redeemer. Father Tom was concerned the casket dolly would not clear the pews as it was moved down the aisle; as a precaution, prior to the funeral he drove to Eagle Harbor, took some measurements, found out there would be three inches of clearance. Mrs. Lamerand was buried from the church she had spent so many years donating her help.

Not long after the exterior vinyl siding was installed (1987), small sections of the north and west walls became detached and blew away, as a result of the fall and winter wind. The original vendor and contractor were requested to review the problem and provide a solution; however, the contractor was no longer in business and the siding vendor blamed faulty installation. Over the next several years siding continued to blow away.

In 2003 Robert Johnson Construction was contracted to replace all exterior vinyl except the east wall. Prior to residing, a 1/2-inch backer board was installed, and the new siding was firmly interlocked to prevent reoccurrence of the former problem. Windows were repaired and the original entrance doors were replaced. The new doors were fabricated by a skilled furniture craftsman who located the same type of white pine used in the original installation, each detail was copied and hand crafted, including a full tenon. They are as close to exact replicas as possible, as those originally installed when Bishop Baraga had the church built in 1854.

Fr. Camillus's Death
In 1988, Father Camillus Hogan O.F.M. became pastor of the Keweenaw Catholic Missions; Father Camillus had served as an assistant at Sacred Heart,

Calumet several years earlier and was happy to be back in the Copper Country. He was interested in electronics and an active member of the local ham radio club. His vehicle of choice, to make the rounds of the scattered churches, was a pickup truck rather than the comfort of an automobile.

The last several years of his ministry here, he had reoccurring medical problems and had occasional confinements in Keweenaw Memorial Hospital, Laurium.

There were times he became ill during Mass and took a few moments to sit down or preach his homily while seated. On one occasion, while celebrating Mass at Holy Redeemer, he fainted and fell to the floor adjacent to the altar. The participating usher rushed to his aid, Father Camillus opened his eyes and said, "Don't help me up, I have to do this myself." After a few apprehensive moments he stood up, shook his head and continued with Mass as if nothing happened.

These medical problems continued to harass him during his tenure. He became ill, after celebrating Mass at Ahmeek, on the morning of 20 December 1994. Someone called the sexton (Donna Dahlgren), who was at work, to inform her that all the parishioners had left but Father was still in the church at 11:00 AM. Donna returned to the church to find him sitting in a chair and too weak to get up. She assisted him to his feet and offered to take him to the rectory, but he insisted on driving himself. Donna followed him to the rectory in Mohawk then persuaded him to seek help at the hospital. Father drove to Keweenaw Memorial about 4:00PM and checked himself in. He was anointed that evening and remained talkative and in good spirits. At about 7:AM the following morning (21 December) he unexpectedly died. His funeral service with Bishop Garland and nine priests present, was held at 11:00 AM on 24 December (Christmas Eve) at Our Lady of Peace Church in Ahmeek. Father Camillus Hogan, O.F.M. is buried in the Franciscan plot at Lake View Cemetery, Calumet.

Father Miles E. Pfalzer, O.F.M. was semi-retired at St. Paul the Apostle in Calumet at the time of Father Camillus's death. The Bishop asked Fr. Miles to take Fr. Camillus's place and was approved by Fr. Miles's provincial. He was officially appointed Administrator of the Keweenaw Catholic Missions in early January 1995.

Father Miles moved to the Mohawk rectory and became active in parish activities.

On 26 May 1997 he celebrated the 50th anniversary of his ordination to the priesthood with the Franciscan Community at Dayton, Ohio.

Electric power came to Eagle Harbor in 1936, subsequently a few electric light fixtures with pull chains, were installed in Holy Redeemer.
In 1998 Father Miles had a new electric service installed; added electric outlets on the east and west side of the sanctuary; a new outlet on the wall adjacent to the organ in the rear of the church; an outlet on the rail up in the choir loft and an interior overhead light at the church entrance.

In the summer of 2001 Father Miles, who was very popular with the Keweenaw and the Calumet parishioners, was the last Franciscan assigned to Keweenaw Catholic Missions. He was transferred to St. Francis Retreat House, Easton, Pennsylvania.

The San Damiano Cross

When the Franciscans left the Keweenaw Catholic Missions in 2001, after 81 years, they presented a San Damiano cross to each area church they had served; at Holy Redeemer the cross is mounted on the west wall of the sanctuary.

The Franciscan Archives of the Province of St. John the Baptist in Cincinnati and Father Ed Lammert, O.F.M provide the following history of the San Damiano cross.

The San Damiano Cross is the one Francis was praying before, when he received the commission from the Lord to rebuild the church. The original cross, fashioned about the year 1100, hangs in Santa Chiara Church in Assisi. In 1257, the Poor Clares moved to Santa Chiara, they took the San Damiano Cross with them and still guard it with great solicitude. The crucifix now hanging over the ancient church of San Damiano is a copy.

All Franciscans cherish this cross as the symbol of their mission from God to commit our lives and resources to renew and rebuild the Church in the power of God.

In the early days after his conversion, Francis was living a penitential life alone in the countryside outside the walls of Assisi. One day, while passing the run-down church known as San Damiano, Francis heard an internal voice from his spirit tell him to go in and pray. He entered and knelt before the cross in contemplation and ecstasy. While gazing at the cross, Francis saw the lips move and heard the words, *"Francis, go repair my house which as you see is falling into ruin."*

At first Francis concentrated on repairing the church buildings of San Damiano and nearby churches. Then when the Lord sent him many followers, he understood his commission to build up the lives of God's people. His commission was confirmed by Pope Innocent III who had a dream of the Church in the form of the Basilica of St. John Lateran leaning as if to fall and one little man holding it from falling.

When the Pope recognized Francis as the little man in his dream, he approved the Franciscan order and its rule of life.

Throughout the centuries the cross has symbolized for Franciscans a mission to bring renewal to the Church.

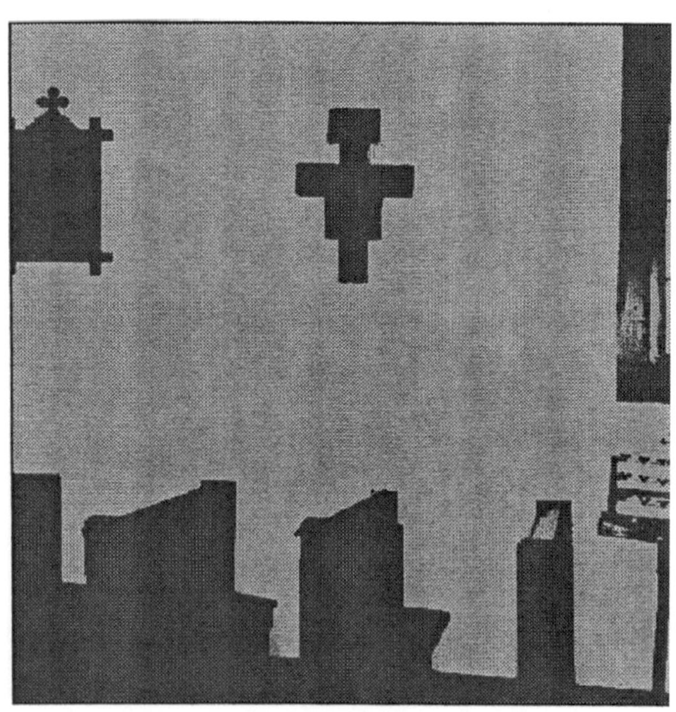

23 San Damiano Cross on west wall
of Holy Redeemer
PHOTO CREDIT: Bob Carlton

22 San Damiano Cross
detail view
PHOTO CREDIT: Franciscan Fathers

Missionary Congregation of the Blessed Sacrament, (M.C.B.S.) 2001-present

In the summer of 2001, Bishop Garland assigned two priests from India and a short time later a third priest, to replace the reassigned Franciscans. All the newly arrived priests belong to the Missionary Congregation of the Blessed Sacrament (MCBS). The order was founded in 1933 at Kerala, India and presently consists of about 157 priests. Christianity was introduced to that part of India by St. Thomas the Apostle in the year 52 AD. The State of Kerala (Land of Coconut) was formed by combining several small regions into one state; at present about 23% of the population are Roman Catholic. Their seminaries are at capacity with a long waiting list for admittance, even though Kerala is one of the smallest states in the Republic of India with an area of 15,000 square miles, which is about one percent of the total land area of India. The three priests are: Father Sebastian Ettolil, pastor, Father Abraham Mupparathara, associate pastor and Father Cyriac Kottayarikil.

They reside at St. Paul the Apostle in Calumet while the rectory at Mohawk remains the Keweenaw Catholic Missions office. Shortly after the arrival of Father Cyriac in Calumet, Father Abraham was transferred to St. Peters Cathedral Parish in Marquette. In the summer of 2003 Father Abraham returned to the area as pastor of Sacred Heart; in the fall of 2003 Father Cyriac was transferred to St. Joseph's in Rudyard, Michigan.

As of 2023, Both Fr. Sebastian and Fr. Cyriac have return to India, and Fr. Sebastian is retired. As of January 2019, Fr. Abraham is the pastor of Holy Redeemer and Holy Spirit parishes in Menominee and Fr. Gracious Pulimootil is the pastor of all parishes in the Keweenaw Catholic Community.

As mentioned earlier, one of Frederic Baraga's first priorities after being appointed Bishop in 1853, was going to Europe for the purpose of recruiting new priests to serve in the Vicariate of the Upper Peninsula. Two young men training for the priesthood in Paris enthusiastically offered their service, but Bishop Baraga reluctantly declined them because both had been trained for the missions in India where he knew some bishop was anxiously awaiting their arrival.

At present, the entire Catholic population of the " Point" from Calumet north, is served by the Missionary Congregation of the Blessed Sacrament from Kerala, India. After a 150-year interval, Bishop Baraga through a successor, Bishop Garland, has blessed us with priests trained in India, who now bring us the Sacraments. This has continued with succeeding Bishops Alexander Sample (now Archbishop of Portland Oregon) and John F. Doerfler.

Buckeye Barracks

Many summer worshippers at Holy Redeemer or Our Lady of the Pines are witness to an announcement by a visiting priest prior to the start of Mass, "Good morning, my name is Father Ed Lammert, I am one of the Buckeye Boys, and have been vacationing here for the past forty years." Fathers Ed and Noel stay at Holy Redeemer rectory and provide Keweenaw Mission priest a reprieve from driving the circuit to Eagle and Copper Harbor during the busy summer season.

In the 1930's a former Calumet resident, Joe Hellner, was a winning basketball and baseball coach at St. Clements Catholic school in St. Bernard (Cincinnati), Ohio. Each summer he would take a group of deserving students to the Copper Country where they camped at an old boarding house in Delaware. The building

Front View   Rear View

24 Buckeye Barracks - Delaware, 1948
PHOTO CREDIT: Fr. Ed Lammert, OFM

was leased from Calumet & Hecla Mining Company for ten dollars per year; the place had no electricity or indoor plumbing, and water was drawn from a nearby well. Each summer the young men would faithfully attend Mass and occupy several pews at Holy Redeemer, and some would serve on the altar as acolytes. The old boarding house was declared unsafe and condemned circa 1950, the lease was terminated on what had been the boys from Ohio summer camp, the Buckeye Barracks. A new building was built at South Point near Lac La Belle and after that, the group attended Mass at Our Lady of the Pines, Copper Harbor.

Father Ed (the former Buckeye Boy) is a Franciscan and resided in Cumberland, Kentucky. He went Home to live with the Lord on 17 December 2016.

Appendix I
Priests assigned to Holy Redeemer Eagle Harbor

*"I have my mission. I may not be told it in this life, but I shall in the next. For I am a link in the chain, a bond of connection between people." ***
By: Venerable John Henry Cardinal Newman 1801-1890

Rev. H.L. Thiele .... 25 October 1854......... 7 October 1862
(Rev. Jacker Interim Nov. 1856 - July 1857)
Rev. Andolschek Interim Apr - Sept. 1861)

Rev. N.J. Konnen .... 5 October 1862........... 5 November 1862

Rev. P.M. Flannigan.............................. 4 November 1862....... 24 August 1863

Rev. John Brown.................................... 4 October 1863........... 24 June 1866
Rev. John Burns .... 19 July 1866............... 15 August 1871
(Interim 5 Months Rev. Jacker)

Rev. A.O. Pelisson .... 19 November 1871...... 29 April 1872

Rev. Luke Mozina................................. 9 June 1872 ....20 July 1877

Rev. A. Paganini .... 1 August 1877............29 October 1979

Rev. Andrew Andolschek....................... 16 November 1879..... until his death
23 June 1882

Rev. Charles Dries .... 20 July 1882...............21 October 1882

Rev. W. Dwyer .... 13 November 1882...... 14 October 1883

Rev. M, Orth.. 4 November 1883 ......8 June 1884

Rev. Edward Jacker............................... 20 July 1884............... 16 May 1886

Rev. Philip Kummert .... May-November 1886

Rev. D. Vento.. Feb-July 1887

Rev. John Henn .... 10 October 1887 ...... 23 Feb. 1888

Rev. C. F. Schelhammer........................ 13 July 1889 .... 3 Sept. 1890
(Interim Apr-May-June Rev. J. Zalokar)

*Cardinal Newman's words submitted by Fr. John McArdle.

Rev. Michael Weis .... 24 September 1890 .. 12 Oct. 1890
Rev. Andrew Henderson O.S.F.............. 2 November 1890 ...... 18 May 1891
Rev. N.H. Nosbisch................................ 12 August 1891 .... 23 Oct. 1892
Rev. A. Molinari .... 12 December 1892 ... 24 Sept. 1893
Rev. A. Mlynarczyk .... 1 December 1893 ..... 4 Feb. 1895

***From this time on, only occasional visits were made to Holy Redeemer
by the following:***
Rev. Angelus O.S.F................................ April 1895
Rev. Paul O.S.F. .... July 1895
Rev. Pakiz... St. Joseph's Calumet
Rev. A. Hodnik....................................... St. Joseph's Calumet
Rev. Sauriol .... Dec. 1895 - Feb. 1896 Lake Linden
Fr. Otto O.S.F.. 8 June 1896 - 29 March 1898
Fr. Peter O.S.F....................................... March 1898
Rev. W.H. Shea...................................... Aug. 1898 - Nov. 1898
Fr. Otto O.S.F.. Spring 1899 - 18 Oct. 1899
Rev. Smietana.. 1899 - 26 February 1902
Rev. Joseph Wvest .... 25 May - 28 December 1902
Rev. W.B. Stahl...................................... 10 Feb. - 7 June 1903
Rev. A. Deschamps .... 30 August 1903 - 12 June 1904
(Last of the regular pastors to serve Holy Redeemer)

Franciscan Fathers - Keweenaw Missions O.F.M.

Friar Pastors: 1905-1963

Alban Schneider

Boniface Klinger

Dunstan Leary

Gabriel Linfert

Benjamin Oehler

Bonaventure Kilfoyle

Juniper Hukenbeck

Clarence Tittel

Jordan Telles

Gerald Held

Other Friars

Ethelbert Harrington

Francis de Paul Lotz

Peter Welling

Otto Ziegler

1978-2001

Faran Boyle .... 1978 - 1984

Matthew Krempel .... 1984 - 1988

Camillus Hogan .... 1988 - 1994

Miles Pfalzer .... 1994 - 2001

Saint Mary's Parish - Mohawk
Including the Keweenaw Missions

Administrator

Fr. John McArdle .... 1963 - 1967

Fr. Donald LaLonde .... 1968 - 1969

Fr. John Chrobak .... 1969 - 1970

Fr. Norman Clisch .... 1970 - 1972

Fr. John Landreville......................... 1972 – 1977

Saint Paul the Apostle Parish
Sacred Heart Parish
Calumet
Including the Keweenaw Missions
Administered by the community of the
Missionary Congregation of the Blessed Sacrament
M.C.B.S.

Fr. Sebastian Ettolil Pastor .... 2001 - 2003

Fr. Abraham Mupparathara .... 2001 - 2002

Fr. Cyriac Kottayarikil..................... 2002 – 2003

Fr. Abraham Mupparathara .... 2003 - 2019

Fr. Gracious Pulimoottil .... 2019 - Present

Serving the Upper Peninsula where needed.

Fr. Tom Schmied O.F.M. Capuchin...................... 1988 - Present

Appendix II
Sample comments from Guest Registration Book

Two guest books were located at the church entrance, one with the first entry date of 26 May 1972 by **Tom Saari-Mohawk, Michigan**: the second one and currently in use, the first entry date 15 September 1990 by **Fr. Camillus Hogan, O.F.M.-Mohawk, Michigan**.

7/27/73	Fr. Paul Proud-homme, SJ St. Stanislaws, Cleveland
7/27/73	Fr. Dan Rupp, O.S.A., Marquette
7/27/73	James A. Hickey, +Rector, North American College, Rome Postulator Apostolic Process of the Baraga Cause.
7/27/73	Charles A. Salatka, Bishop Marquette

8/-/73   Mark Spreitzer..*Former summer organist here. Good to see church is the same.*

8/25/73   Mr.& Mrs. John Wakeman, Hibbing, MM ....*17th wedding anniversary in this church.*

10/6/73   Donald MacDonald III, Negaunee, MI ....*My relatives Mr.& Mrs. Donald MacDonald were married here in 1866.*

6/-/74   Fr. Stanley Poderzat, SJ Slovenian....................*Beautiful, inspired by Missionary in Calcutta, India   Baraga's example.*

8/-/75   Margaret Long Renner, Fargo, ND ....*My grandparents were one of the first couples married here.*

8/24/75   Mr.& Mrs. F.J. Beyers, Soo, MI ....*Married in this church 8/24/31.*

6/27/76   Mr.& Mrs.Robert Baril, Lake Linden...............*Glad to visit the church my grandparents were married in.*

7/2/78   Anna Stiglich Orlando, FL................................*My mother and dad were married in the blessed church 5/8/1901.*

8/5/78   Cy & Martha Fortier, Iron Mt, MI ....*Came to see carpeting donated in memory of our mother, love this church.*

9/4/79   St.Arnold's Westland, MI..................................*Mother and father were married here 104 years ago.*

+Later elevated to Cardinal and Archbishop of Washington D.C., July 1980 - Nov. 2000.

A

| 8/4/84 | Theodore and Chancellor Hicks | *Twin boys baptized here today.* |

8/4/84   Theodore and Chancellor Hicks ....*Twin boys baptized here today.*

8/4/87   Florence (Lamerand) Brown Manistique, MI.........*sang in the choir here in 1935.*

7/12/91   Signed by 20 members of Malnar family ....*Mr. & Mrs. Anton Malnar married here in 1901 our parents and grandparents.*

8/10/91   First recorded guitar Mass sung in this church .....*Performed by Elizabeth, Dayton and Pug Hicks, Bob Masnado and Nancy (Masnado) Bloch.*

10/9/92   Jean & Bob Goetz St. Louis, MO ....*Lovely church, but where are the Trappist Monks that make jelly?*

8/8/93   Jeanne DiMario Rockford,IL ....*I am in Awe! This church represents a true living faith! God Bless all those who work to preserve this house of God. Thank you.*

8/14/94   Bob & Peg Carlton, Eagle Harbor ....*Renewed wedding vows 50th anniversary by Fr. Camillus Hogan OFM.*

6/30/97   28 names on one page, all from Slovenia ....*Beautiful church, thank you for having it open.*

7/15/91   Fr. Henry Maibusch, OSA ....*May God grant Beatification and Sainthood to Bp. Baraga.*
         Holy Rosary Church, Kenosha,WI

8/4/98   Sr. Jelaine Jaeb OSU, St. Louis, MO.....................*It was thrilling to see relics of Sts Angela & Ursula the founder & patroness Ursuline Order to which I belong.*

8/9/98   Alice Helwig, Marquette......................................*Our mother crocheted the altar cloths here.*
         Shirley Keir, Laurium

9/22/98   Lois Stevens (LaBine) DeMarois...........................*My great-grandparents were the first couple married in this church.*

8/30/99   Fr. Philip R. Smith, C.P.P.S. Rome, Italy ....*Che Bella! Grazie!*
         Secretary General Missionaries of the
         Precious Blood

B

9/10/01   Mary & Dan Turvey, Marquette ....*A friend, now 90 yrs. old, as a child, used to bring wildflowers here to the to the church, the tradition has survived.*

7/13/02 Fr.Krajuc Ljubljana, Slovenia ....*We are a group from Slovenia,* and a group of bicyclers   *(the homeland of Baraga) following in his footsteps cycling to the places he visited. We will then go to Toronto to meet thousands.*

7/2/03   Vera Shuty Pischiattino, West Allis, WI...............*Precious memory, went to this church as a young girl in 1936.*

7/9/03   Harold and Beu Bell Livonia, MI ....*Harold's mother was baptized here in 1913. Brought our children here to see it.*

There are over four thousand entries in the Guest Books kept from 1972 until 2023, by far the most repetitive theme is "Thank you" for having the church open so we may spend a few moments in prayer and golden memories, within the solitude of this simple church, Bishop Baraga built so many years ago.

www.ingramcontent.com/pod-product-compliance
Lightning Source LLC
Chambersburg PA
CBHW042044110726
48006CB00002B/283